Guion and Friends

A Creative Activity Book

The sun rises on the savanna.

COLOR BY NUMBER
Use the color key below to color in the picture.

DRAW FROM IMAGINATION

Look at these common objects. If you squint your eyes and
use your imagination, what else could they be? Draw your vision.

CREATIVITY
TAKES
COURAGE
-Henri Matisse

FINISH THE DRAWING

Help Rae finish the drawing
of the castle below.

FINISH THE DRAWING

What does Hoke see floating on the water?
Is there anything below the surface?
Draw what you imagine!

BURIED TREASURE

If you found a buried treasure, what
would you hope was in it? Draw it!

DESIGN A T-SHIRT
Create an original T-shirt design for Hoke.

COMIC STRIP

Come up with a short story about Guion the Lion and his friend Rae the Bushbaby. Tell your story with pictures below. Write what they are saying in the speech bubbles.

MIRROR REFLECTION

Draw the mirror reflection (upside down)
of Hoke and Wilson at the watering hole.

DRAWING WITH SHAPES

Turn these circles and semi-circles into Guion the Lion.

DRAWING WITH SHAPES

Connect these squares to make Wilson the Giraffe.

POSTCARD FROM PARADISE

Where is paradise to you? The ocean, the mountains, the savanna where Guion and his friends live, or maybe your idea of the perfect vacation is a visit to ride the world's best roller coaster? Draw a picture of your own personal paradise.

POSTCARD FROM PARADISE

Make up a story about something you would like to do in your own personal paradise and write a message about it to a friend or family member.

POSTCARD

GRID DRAWING

Use this picture key to copy the dragon in the grid below.

The T-Rex guards her nest.

THINK BELIEVE DREAM AND DARE

DESIGN A PATTERN
Draw a unique pattern for Wilson the Giraffe.

Savanna Spotlight

Sunday   Vol. 12, No. 2

T-Rex spotted at volcano crater!

WRITE A NEWS HEADLINE FOR THIS IMAGE.

I CAN DO HARD THINGS
I AM BRAVE
LIFE IS TOUGH, BUT SO AM I
EVERY DAY IS AN ADVENTURE
I AM KIND
I AM ONE OF A KIND
I KEEP GOING
I HAVE BIG DREAMS

DESIGN BUTTONS
Use the positive statements on the
left to design some cool buttons below.

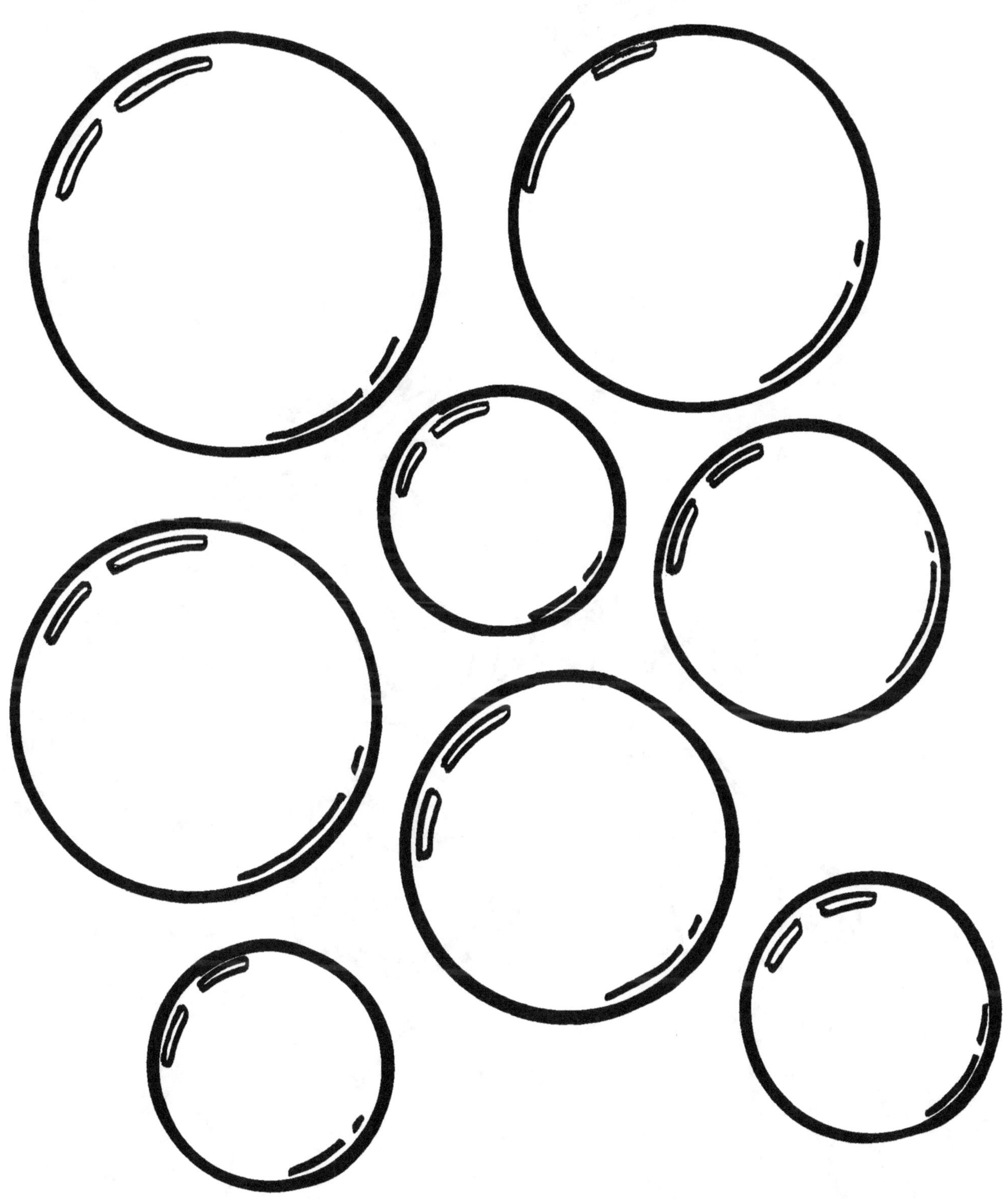

CONNECT THE CONSTELLATIONS

Connect the stars by numbers and letters to form constellations.

CONNECT THE CONSTELLATIONS

Connect the stars by numbers and letters to form constellations.

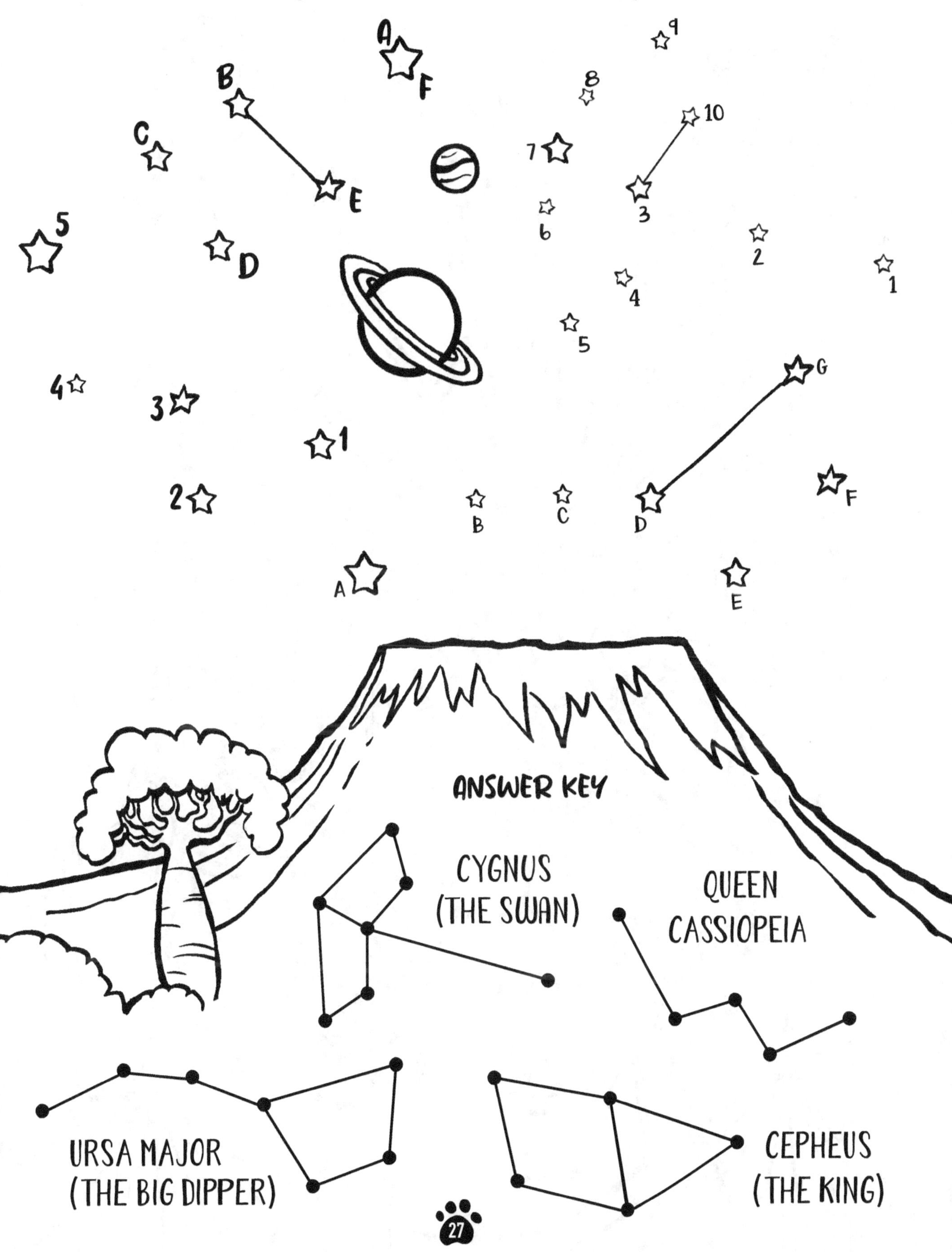

The best days...

Are even better with friends.

TANGRAM PUZZLES
Use the puzzle pieces on the next page to recreate Guion and Friends out of tangram puzzle pieces.

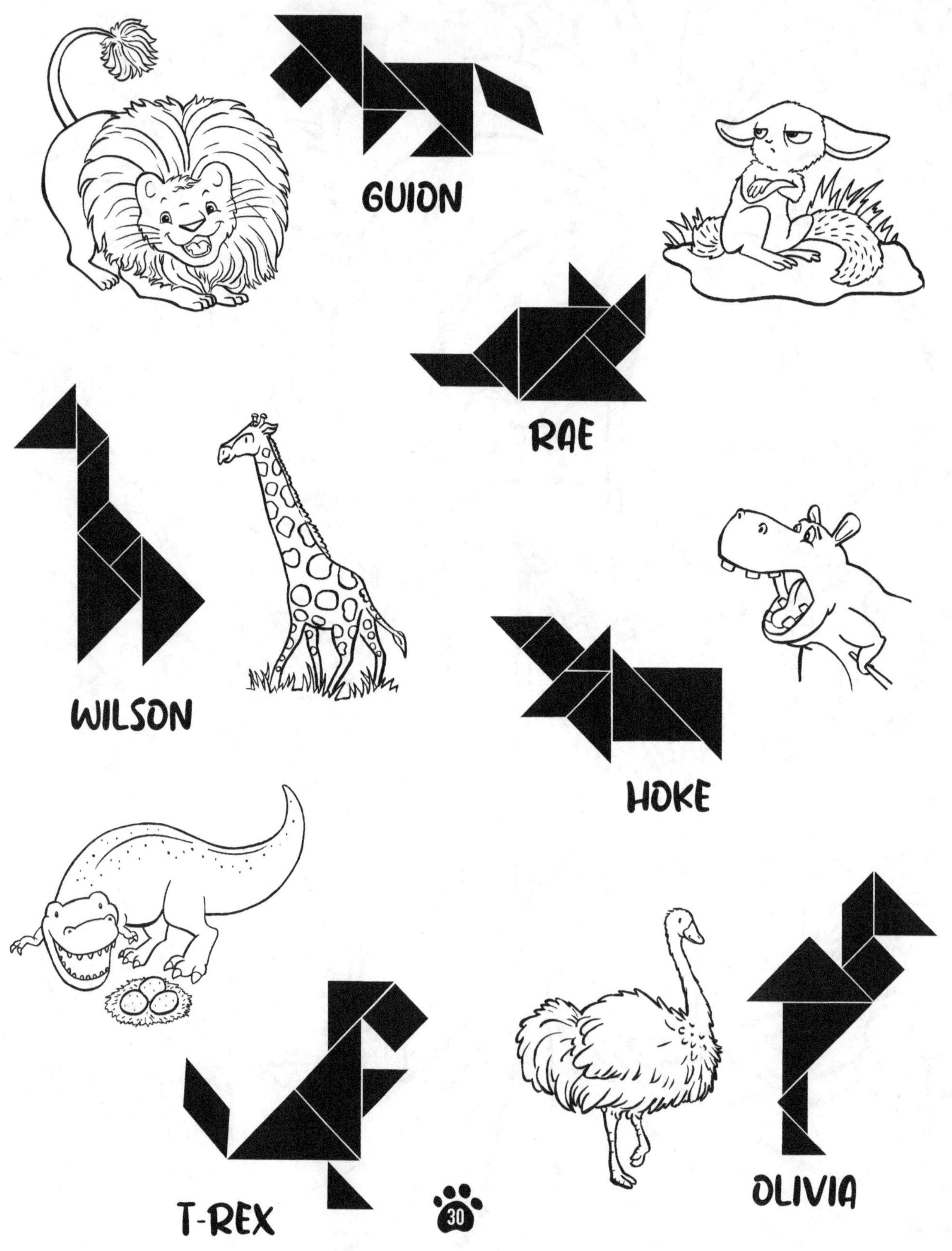

TANGRAM PUZZLE PIECES
Ask an adult to help you cut out the seven tangram pieces.

BLANK PAGE REQUESTED BY MANUFACTURER